Public Outreach and Participation

John B. Stephens
Ricardo S. Morse
Kelley T. O'Brien

UNC
SCHOOL OF
GOVERNMENT

About the Series

Local Government Board Builders offers local elected leaders practical advice on how to effectively lead and govern. Each of the booklets in this series provides a topic overview, specific tips on effective practice, and worksheets and reflection questions to help local elected leaders improve their work. The series focuses on common activities for local governing boards, such as selecting and appointing committees and advisory boards, planning for the future, making better decisions, improving board accountability, and effectively engaging stakeholders in public decisions.

Vaughn Mamlin Upshaw, lecturer in public administration and government at the UNC School of Government, is the series editor.

Other Books in the Series

Leading Your Governing Board: A Guide for Mayors and County Board Chairs,
Vaughn Mamlin Upshaw, 2009

A Model Code of Ethics for North Carolina Local Elected Officials,
A. Fleming Bell, II, 2010

Creating and Maintaining Effective Local Government Citizen Advisory Committees,
Vaughn Mamlin Upshaw, 2010

Working with Nonprofit Organizations,
Margaret Henderson, Lydian Altman, Suzanne Julian, Gordon P. Whitaker,
Eileen R. Youens, 2010

Local Government Revenue Sources in North Carolina,
Kara A. Millonzi, forthcoming in 2011

The School of Government at the University of North Carolina at Chapel Hill works to improve the lives of North Carolinians by engaging in practical scholarship that helps public officials and citizens understand and improve state and local government. Established in 1931 as the Institute of Government, the School provides educational, advisory, and research services for state and local governments. The School of Government is also home to a nationally ranked graduate program in public administration and specialized centers focused on information technology, environmental finance, and civic education for youth.

As the largest university-based local government training, advisory, and research organization in the United States, the School of Government offers up to 200 courses, seminars, and specialized conferences for more than 12,000 public officials each year. In addition, faculty members annually publish approximately fifty books, book chapters, bulletins, and other reference works related to state and local government. Each day that the General Assembly is in session, the School produces the *Daily Bulletin*, which reports on the day's activities for members of the legislature and others who need to follow the course of legislation.

The Master of Public Administration Program is a full-time, two-year program that serves up to sixty students annually. It consistently ranks among the best public administration graduate programs in the country, particularly in city management. With courses ranging from public policy analysis to ethics and management, the program educates leaders for local, state, and federal governments and nonprofit organizations.

Operating support for the School of Government's programs and activities comes from many sources, including state appropriations, local government membership dues, private contributions, publication sales, course fees, and service contracts. Visit www .sog.unc.edu or call 919.966.5381 for more information on the School's courses, publications, programs, and services.

Michael R. Smith, DEAN
Thomas H. Thornburg, SENIOR ASSOCIATE DEAN
Frayda S. Bluestein, ASSOCIATE DEAN FOR FACULTY DEVELOPMENT
Todd A. Nicolet, ASSOCIATE DEAN FOR OPERATIONS
Ann Cary Simpson, ASSOCIATE DEAN FOR DEVELOPMENT AND COMMUNICATIONS
Bradley G. Volk, ASSOCIATE DEAN FOR ADMINISTRATION

FACULTY

Gregory S. Allison
David N. Ammons
Ann M. Anderson
A. Fleming Bell, II
Maureen M. Berner
Mark F. Botts
Michael Crowell
Shea Riggsbee Denning
James C. Drennan
Richard D. Ducker
Joseph S. Ferrell
Alyson A. Grine

Norma Houston
Cheryl Daniels Howell
Jeffrey A. Hughes
Willow S. Jacobson
Robert P. Joyce
Kenneth L. Joyner
Diane M. Juffras
Dona G. Lewandowski
James M. Markham
Janet Mason
Christopher B. McLaughlin
Laurie L. Mesibov

Kara A. Millonzi
Jill D. Moore
Jonathan Q. Morgan
Ricardo S. Morse
C. Tyler Mulligan
David W. Owens
William C. Rivenbark
Dale J. Roenigk
John Rubin
Jessica Smith
Karl W. Smith
Carl W. Stenberg III

John B. Stephens
Charles Szypszak
Shannon H. Tufts
Vaughn Upshaw
Aimee N. Wall
Jeffrey B. Welty
Richard B. Whisnant
Gordon P. Whitaker
Eileen R. Youens

© 2011
School of Government
The University of North Carolina at Chapel Hill

Use of this publication for commercial purposes or without acknowledgment of its source is prohibited. Reproducing, distributing, or otherwise making available to a non-purchaser the entire publication, or a substantial portion of it, without express permission, is prohibited.

Printed in the United States of America
21 20 19 18 17   2 3 4 5 6
ISBN 978-1-56011-659-2

Contents

Introduction

City and county elected officials hear from their constituents all the time. Yet there is often confusion about how public participation* occurs and how it affects decision making by municipal and county boards. This guide provides specific ideas for

- When and how to engage the public
- What to think about in designing a variety of participation mechanisms, such as surveys, hearings, and community meetings
- How to be more inclusive, regardless of what participation method is used
- How to develop long-term community participation by partnering with civic organizations and involving youth in local government

Public officials need to think beyond particular tools to the broader plan for what they want to accomplish through various types of public participation. All the tips in this guide depend on officials' goals and visions for informed, involved residents in their communities.

This guide covers common forms of structured participation, such as citizen comment periods at regular city council or county commission meetings and public hearings. It notes some higher-tech possibilities such as using social media. It offers practical guidance on both traditional and innovative ways of involving the public.

Part 1 focuses on the big picture: the whys, whens, and hows of public participation. It examines several issues public leaders should consider in choosing among various participation methods. Part 2 offers practical tips for disseminating information and engaging the public.

---

*Almost all North Carolina communities have residents who are not U.S. citizens. Community leaders choose to what degree these noncitizens can and should participate in local decision making. References to "public participation" in this publication should be taken to mean participation by all residents of a city or county, regardless of citizenship status. Terms such as "citizens academy" and "citizen advisory committee" should also be considered inclusive of all members of a community.

A separate Board Builders publication, *Creating and Maintaining Effective Local Government Citizen Advisory Committees*, by Vaughn Mamlin Upshaw, focuses on city council–appointed advisory committees and county and regional advisory boards.

PART 1
The Big Picture on Public Participation

The Whys of Public Participation

Campaigns and elections aside, people in communities can and do participate in community governance in a variety of ways. One of public officials' responsibilities is to choose when and how a local government encourages participation. These decisions are based on the reasons officials think public participation is important or necessary. If officials don't have clear reasons for the choices they make, those choices are unlikely to lead to satisfactory results. Residents in the community and other interested stakeholders also make choices about whether to participate—and in what ways—based on their own reasons. Some of the common reasons why government leaders encourage public participation and residents choose to participate in local government are discussed below. These reasons are summarized in Table 1.

Local Governments' Reasons for Involving the Public

From a government official's perspective, a fundamental reason for involving the public is that it is required by law. Open meetings law mandates opportunities for the public to participate in local government meetings as observers. Required public comment periods provide members of the public the opportunity to speak to the board. Certain actions by local government boards, such as passing budgets, require formal public hearings. Therefore, all local board members are legally required to have public observation and input, at least at certain times.

Beyond legal mandates, a general sense of obligation to participate in government is rooted in the democratic values of the United States. Most public officials believe that citizens have the right to be involved in the governance of their communities. At question is the nature and extent of participation. Most local leaders try to build trust with residents so that people voicing their opinions do not feel unheard or unappreciated. Leaders usually envision serving the whole community rather than only those constituents who agree with them or who supported them at election time. However, these inclusive and

Table 1.   Reasons for Public Participation in Local Government

Government Perspective	Citizen/Resident Perspective
Required by law	Clear interest in the matter and want to influence the decision because they are directly affected by it
Citizens have a right to be involved	
Allows better understanding of problems	Civic responsibility and general interest in community well-being
Introduces fresh ideas on options	
Ensures better decisions and outcomes	Personal satisfaction
Creates a sense of community representation	Special expertise to contribute
Encourages greater buy-in and political cover	Personal ambition
Gets message out to community	
Allows transparency and helps build trust	
Helps build long-term capacity for community problem solving	

democratic values often clash with the practicalities of time, resources, and level of public interest in the details of local government.

Local officials may seek public participation out of a desire to better understand the nature of problems or issues they face. They realize that their perspective is limited and that constituents may offer other perspectives. As well, the public may have fresh ideas for possible solutions. Involving the public may enable the government to make better decisions and produce more favorable outcomes.

Government leaders may also recognize that communities are not perfectly represented by their elected boards. Seeking input from the public results in a process that is as inclusive as possible.

Public participation is also a proactive way for public officials to generate buy-in for tough decisions the board has to make. If the public is involved—even if a decision has some detractors—the council's action may be seen as more legitimate and therefore more acceptable due to the process having been open and fair. Some officials use the term "political cover" to describe an open, transparent, participatory process that allows difficult decisions to be defended by pointing to the fairness of the process.

A related reason for inviting public participation is that doing so provides an opportunity for the government to get its message out to the community. Being proactive can generate support for (or at least acceptance of) tough decisions that might otherwise be unfairly criticized because the public did not have the complete story.

Public participation can be viewed as a component of greater transparency and openness in government. With national polls showing that trust in government is declining or holding steady at low levels,[1] increased transparency, openness, and participation can be a strategy to help improve trust in government. A related long-term benefit of public participation is that it can be seen as building capacity within a community for citizens to work together to solve problems. People with different viewpoints who choose to work productively with their government are assets to be leveraged during future tough times.

Citizens' Reasons for Getting Involved

Citizens have their own reasons for participating in the governance process. First and foremost is the desire to be involved in decisions that have a direct impact on them. If citizens feel that an issue addressed by local government directly affects their lives, property, or needed services, they are likely to want to have a say in that decision.

Many people consider it their civic responsibility to be involved in their communities. They have a strong commitment to the general welfare of the community and feel obligated to take part in opportunities to participate beyond voting in elections. Additionally, some residents get personal satisfaction out of participating in government affairs.

Sometimes people have special expertise or training that they want to share. They may be involved out of a sense of professional duty. These people can be valuable contributors to the public process, providing information and suggesting options that local government and the general public might not be aware of.

Finally, some people may choose to participate out of personal ambition. They may have plans to seek elected or appointed office and view public participation in local government as a step in that direction.

When designing public participation, it is important to be clear about local government's motivations and the public's needs and concerns. Being open and honest about those motivations will help clarify when and how the public should be invited to participate.

Why Local Governments May Choose Not to Invite Participation

Just as it is important to consider the reasons why local governments might seek public participation and the reasons individuals might choose to participate, it is also important to examine possible reasons for nonparticipation. These reasons are summarized in Table 2.

Table 2. Reasons for Nonparticipation

Government Perspective	Citizen/Resident Perspective
Contrast between professional, rational expertise and irrational input	Competing demands for time
Silent majority not represented	Not able to participate due to meeting schedule or other circumstances
More efficient—saves time and money	Do not see direct impact
Potential for getting burned	Do not believe participation will make a difference
Loss of control	Out of comfort zone
Accountability issues	

In spite of the benefits derived from public participation, there are several reasons why inviting public participation may make officials nervous. First, there is an ethos of professionalism in local government, particularly in the council–manager and commission–manager forms of government that predominate in North Carolina. Well-trained staff members apply their expertise and seek rational solutions. Participation by citizens is sometimes viewed as emotional and irrational. Local government leaders may believe that their higher level of informed, reasoned analysis will produce outcomes for the good of the whole community, while individual residents' poorly informed and narrow input will not.

In discussions of public participation, it is common to refer to the so-called silent majority. Usually, only a few residents get involved in a given issue, and their opinions may represent only the extreme points of view on either side of the issue. The silent majority, on the other hand, is generally assumed to agree with the local government's stance on the issue and thus does not get involved. There are, of course, problems with these assumptions, as discussed below.

Public officials may also be concerned about the time and cost involved in public participation. Inviting participation may be viewed as reducing government efficiency and wasting valuable time and money. However, what appears to be a consensus that supports quick, efficient action may lead to unexpected opposition. In that case, it may take less time and fewer resources overall to involve the public from the very beginning.

Public officials sometimes fear that inviting public participation increases the risk of conflict. There are many stories of governments inviting participation only to end up with more controversy and unrest than they expected.

Finally, inviting participation may be viewed as giving up control. Elected officials are chosen to represent constituents and make decisions on their behalf. They may rightly be concerned about turning over some aspects of the decision making process to unelected, self-selected participants or allowing the opinions of a small group of residents to influence official decisions that have a broad impact.

Why Citizens May Choose Not to Participate

City and county residents have their own reasons for not getting involved. Sometimes local government officials assume apathy, when in fact there are many valid reasons why people choose not to participate.

One primary reason for lack of participation is the time it requires. People may simply be too busy with work, family, or leisure activities to attend meetings. They may have the desire to participate, but their work schedules are incompatible with meeting schedules. Or they may lack transportation to meetings.

In other cases, people fail to make the connection between participation in local government and their daily lives. They do not see how their involvement will affect them. Many public decisions, though important, fail to generate a sense of urgency among citizens. In order for people to desire to participate, they usually need to be personally concerned about the issue and have a sense that their participation will make a difference.

Finally, many people choose not to participate because doing so is out of their comfort zone. Some may fear public events and having to speak up. Others may fear retribution. There may also be barriers—either real or perceived—that make participation seem too difficult (for example, concern over one's English-speaking skills, or a physical disability).

Whatever the concern, it is important for board members to be aware of and confront their own and their staff members' biases against participation. Additionally, when planning for participation, it is imperative to consider why people often choose not to participate and to address those concerns, if possible.

WORKSHEET: *Setting Goals and Steps for Effective Public Participation*

Why does our local government involve the public?

_____
_____
_____
_____

What are the benefits of this involvement?

_____
_____
_____
_____

What are the costs?

_____
_____
_____
_____

In what ways does the public want to be involved in our local government?

_____
_____
_____
_____

How successful have we been in getting the public involved? What works best in our community?

_____
_____
_____
_____

Timing of Public Participation

Decisions over *how* to involve the public should be preceded by the fundamental question of *when* to do so. Public discontent over opportunities to participate is often based on the belief that a decision has already been made. The public may view a participatory process as illegitimate, or at least not worthwhile, if they have been brought in too late in the process.

In thinking about what is too late or too early or just right, it is helpful to understand the steps involved in making policies and taking action—known as the "policy cycle." First, a set of conditions is identified as a problem. Next, criteria for evaluating the problem are determined and options for solving the problem are identified and weighed against the criteria. A decision is then made and implemented. Afterward, the results of the policy decision are evaluated in some way, which often leads to the identification of a new problem (or opportunity).

The policy cycle set forth in Figure 1 is general and ideal. In actual practice there is much variation; problems are not always clearly defined, evaluative criteria may not be explicitly discussed, and so forth. The different phases of the policy cycle are almost always present in some form, however, as governments go about making decisions.

The policy cycle can be useful in considering when to invite public participation. Staff members usually do the background work of defining the problem, selecting the evaluation criteria, and identifying options. They often perform some kind of analysis of the options. The elected board then receives the recommendations and may seek the public's input as it weighs the options. A local budget hearing is an example of this type of public input. In a budget hearing, citizens are invited to comment on a mostly finished product. The board hears the citizens, then deliberates and makes decisions (often in the same evening).

Is this appropriate timing for public participation, or is it too late? How might public participation in the budget process, for example, work if people participated earlier? Citizen advisory boards are one example of a participation mechanism designed to bring the public into the policy cycle much earlier. If it is established early enough, an advisory

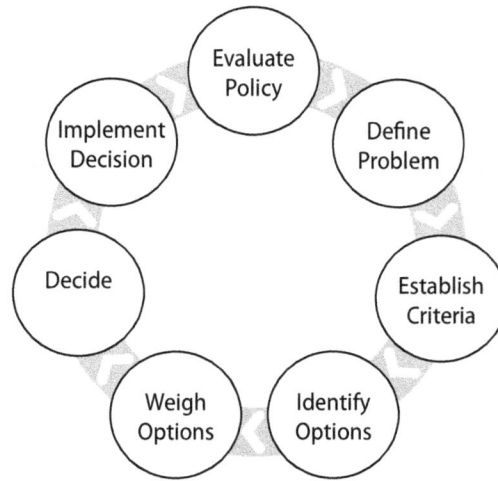

Figure 1. The Policy Cycle—Numerous scholars of public policy have represented the policy process in terms of a cycle or stages. This representation of the policy cycle is adapted from Wayne Parsons, *Public Policy: An Introduction to the Theory and Practice of Policy Analysis* (Northampton, MA: Edward Elgar, 1995).

board can play a role in framing the problem, establishing evaluation criteria, identifying options, and so forth.[2]

Other participation models invite participation in the later phases of the policy cycle: implementation and evaluation. Participation in implementing policies of local government can take the form of client feedback and even coproduction (see sidebar on page 13). For example, recreation programs usually involve a great deal of coordination between government employees and volunteer coaches. The users of facilities and team programs provide feedback to recreation officials. Volunteer coaches coproduce a public service, recreation, with a local government agency. Municipal curbside recycling programs also involve a policy that depends on active involvement of residents, who must sort their disposables into the appropriate recycling bins. During the evaluation phase, surveys may be used to assess satisfaction with local government programs and policies. Some local governments have also experimented with in-depth performance assessments provided by community members.

Coproduction

Public participation is usually thought of in terms of engaging people in the public decision making process. But in several areas, implementing government programs depends on specific, supportive actions by residents. In other words, citizens can be partners with their local governments in delivering public services. Some examples include

- Neighborhood Watch programs
- Volunteer positions within public programs (for example, recreation programs or libraries)
- Volunteer fire departments
- Adopt-a-Highway or Adopt-a-Park programs
- Community festivals

There is no formula to determine the best time to invite public participation. In general, however, the earlier participation is sought, the greater the chance that the participation will be seen as meaningful by those involved. It is wise to avoid the perception of inviting participation when, for all intents and purposes, the decision has already been made.

WORKSHEET: *Inviting Participation*

When do we typically ask the public to participate in the decision making cycle?

_____
_____
_____
_____

What are the advantages and disadvantages of engaging the public at this point in the process?

_____
_____
_____
_____

How to Involve the Public: Breadth versus Depth

The extent of public participation is often dictated by *how many people* local government wants to try to reach (breadth) and *how substantive* the participation will be in terms of time, involvement, and impact (depth).

Breadth refers to how large a proportion of the community is involved (or at least has the opportunity to be involved). A survey that goes to each household in the community, for example, would score very high for breadth because virtually everyone in the community would have the opportunity to participate. However, the survey would reflect only what residents were thinking at the moment, and their opinions could change if they were given the opportunity to study the issue.

Depth, on the other hand, refers to how deeply involved participants will be and how great an impact their participation will have. An advisory committee, for example, would not allow many people to participate, but those who were involved would need to devote a great deal of time and effort, and they would also expect their participation to have a greater impact. The committee would therefore score low on breadth but high on depth. Greater depth will almost always mean that fewer citizens are able to participate.

Figure 2 illustrates the depth versus breadth of some common public participation tools. Many of these public participation tools are referenced in the Appendix.

As suggested by the idea of breadth, there are different levels of public participation—from keeping the public informed to empowering citizens to make final decisions. Figure 3, the IAP2 Spectrum of Public Participation, provides examples of public participation goals, the promises to the public (implicit or explicit) inherent in each goal, and examples of techniques for achieving the goal.

Referenda

Surveys

Websites and
Social Media

Study Circles

Community Meetings

Public Hearings

Public
Comment
Periods

Task Forces

Citizen Boards

Inform   Consult   Involve   Collaborate   Empower

BREADTH
(Increasing Amount of Public Access)

DEPTH
(Increasing Level of Public Impact)

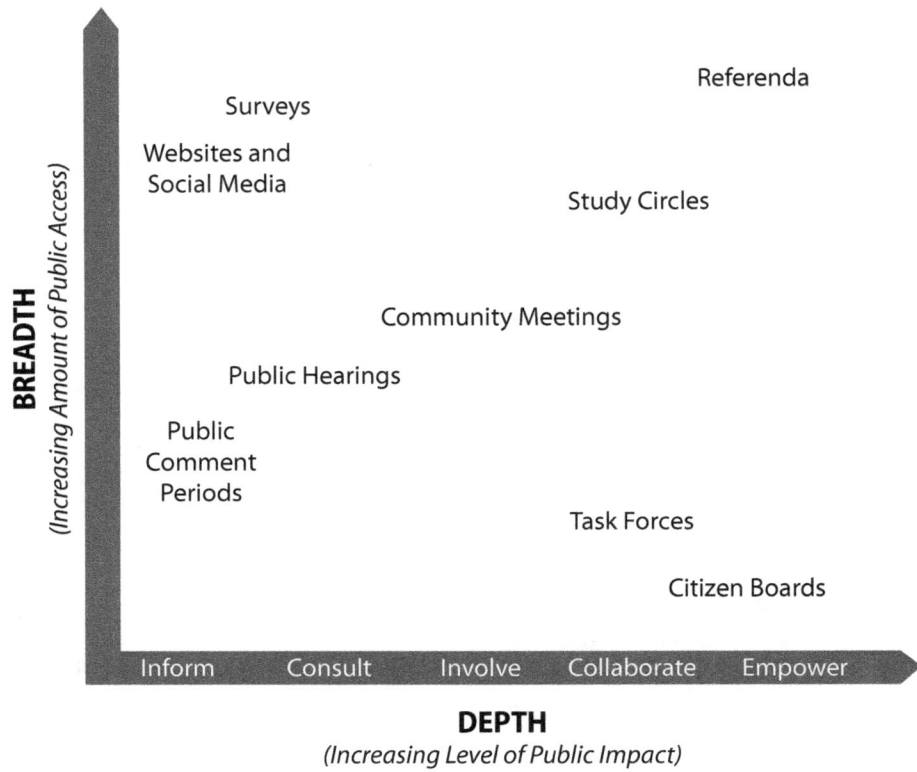

Source: Ricardo S. Morse, UNC School of Government, 2010

Figure 2.   Public Participation—Depth versus Breadth

IAP2 Spectrum
of Public Participation

iap2
International Association
for Public Participation

Increasing Level of Public Impact →

	Inform	Consult	Involve	Collaborate	Empower
Public participation goal	To provide the public with balanced and objective information to assist them in understanding the problem, alternatives, opportunities and/or solutions.	To obtain public feedback on analysis, alternatives and/or decisions.	To work directly with the public throughout the process to ensure that public concerns and aspirations are consistently understood and considered.	To partner with the public in each aspect of the decision including the development of alternatives and the identification of the preferred solution.	To place final decision-making in the hands of the public.
Promise to the public	We will keep you informed.	We will keep you informed, listen to and acknowledge concerns and aspirations, and provide feedback on how public input influenced the decision.	We will work with you to ensure that your concerns and aspirations are directly reflected in the alternatives developed and provide feedback on how public input influenced the decision.	We will look to you for advice and innovation in formulating solutions and incorporate your advice and recommendations into the decisions to the maximum extent possible.	We will implement what you decide.
Example techniques	■ Fact sheets ■ Web sites ■ Open houses	■ Public comment ■ Focus groups ■ Surveys ■ Public meetings	■ Workshops ■ Deliberative polling	■ Citizen advisory committees ■ Consensus-building ■ Participatory decision-making	■ Citizen juries ■ Ballots ■ Delegated decision

Figure 3. IAP2 Spectrum of Public Participation

WORKSHEET: *Considering the How of Participation*

Which of our public participation approaches add breadth? Which approaches add depth?

_____

_____

_____

_____

Have there been times when we needed breadth and used depth, or vice versa? What happened, and how did our choice influence the outcomes for the local government board and the community?

_____

_____

_____

_____

How does the nature of an issue influence the extent to which we seek breadth and depth in participation?

_____

_____

_____

_____

Effective Outreach to All Parts of the Community

Officials often are concerned when a small, motivated, well-organized group of citizens, which may not be representative of the wider community, receives media attention. While people who care passionately about a matter deserve to be heard, the sentiments of the general community must also be considered. Public officials may need to think of a variety of ways to reach people—particularly those who have limited ability to participate due to age, physical disability, language barriers, work schedules, or family demands.

One basic but important step for encouraging public participation is to use commonly understood language if at all possible. Terms that are commonly used in local government meetings and printed materials—such as *capital budget, consent agenda, motion to amend, and performance measurement*—may be unfamiliar to some constituents and can be viewed as "government speak" (that is, language that is intentionally difficult to understand).

Governments often create unintentional barriers for marginalized groups of people. These may take many forms, including the following:

- *Language.* Many residents do not speak English as their first language. The use of technical language can also impede understanding.

- *Assumptions of knowledge.* Governments often entertain incorrect assumptions about people's life experience, knowledge of an issue, knowledge of legal standards and regulations, and general knowledge of how government works.

- *Simple logistics.* Some residents may have transportation or child care issues, irregular work schedules, or physical disabilities that prevent them from effectively participating in meetings. It is important for the physical space for participation to be seen as safe and accessible for all residents and other stakeholders.

- *Meeting format and organizational structure.* Residents who are unfamiliar with common meeting formats—for example, the use of *Roberts Rules of Order*—may not feel as though they are able to participate fully.

With some forethought and consideration, local governments can be much more open and welcoming and therefore more likely to reach those not inclined to be involved in community matters.

WORKSHEET: *Reducing Barriers*

What barriers to participation does our local government create?

_____

_____

_____

_____

How have these barriers become visible to us?

_____

_____

_____

What can we do to remove them?

_____

_____

_____

_____

Public Participation Methods

Public participation occurs in many ways. As elected officials well know, other people often initiate the contact. Conversations on public issues occur when elected officials are shopping or in restaurants or other public spaces. Residents contact elected officials individually through phone calls and e-mail.

In contrast, public hearings and comment periods during governing board meetings are official ways for eliciting public input. They are predictable aspects of government decision making that allow people to provide their input to the full board.

Once a local government has a clear picture of the ways it seeks or responds to public participation, that information may be used to consider how well the tools work to reach the whole community.

✐ WORKSHEET: *Identifying Individual and Community Participation*

Check all activities in which you participate:

Often	Sometimes	Seldom or Never	Public Participation Method
○	○	○	Citizen comment periods at board meetings (required by law for at least one meeting per month)
○	○	○	Public hearings (some are required by law, but many cities/counties choose to hold hearings on a variety of concerns)
○	○	○	Phone calls from individual constituents
○	○	○	People talking to you at public events or in public places
○	○	○	E-mails (individual e-mails to you or mass e-mails to the whole board)
○	○	○	Surveys (written, Internet, telephone, etc.)

○ ○ ○	○ ○ ○	○ ○ ○	Neighborhood meetings
			    On a regular basis
			    Only on specific topics

○	○	○	Cable TV—government or public access channel
○	○	○	Radio call-in shows
○	○	○	Meetings of civic, social, business, or professional groups
○	○	○	Letters
○	○	○	Petitions
○	○	○	Citizen advisory committees
○	○	○	Community meetings or roundtable discussions (may address a city/county concern but are not conducted by a statutory public body)
○	○	○	Blogs
○	○	○	Facebook (for your city/county, not a personal/private account)
○	○	○	Twitter
○	○	○	Other

Engaging the Whole Community

It is often easiest to hear from a few residents and from organized interest groups. The challenge is to supplement these views with those from less-active community members. Three segments of the community that are particularly challenging to reach are youth, older residents, and people who are frequently away from home or have irregular work schedules. The following sections present some ideas for reaching those residents.

Youth

According to the U.S. Census Bureau's 2006–2008 American Community Survey, 24.3 percent of North Carolina's population is under the age of 18. Providing young people opportunities to voice their opinions on government decisions is an important mechanism for creating a community of engaged residents and future leaders.

When seeking the viewpoints of youth in a community, it is important to design meaningful, genuine opportunities. Soliciting youth feedback should not be tokenism; officials should be prepared to consider the feedback and explain how the young people's involvement affected their decisions.

Youth councils are one mechanism for soliciting young people's feedback in an ongoing, meaningful, and genuine manner. A youth council is an advisory body composed of local young people (usually high school–aged) who provide advice and counsel to the local governing body and its affiliated advisory and regulatory boards, as well as to other community organizations.

Youth councils enable young people to

- Communicate their concerns regarding local matters that affect them
- Directly participate in local government
- Make decisions and take action to improve their communities

Youth councils enable local councils/boards of commissioners to

- Be more representative of the community as a whole
- Gain insight into young people's perspectives
- Encourage young people to be more actively engaged in their communities
- Improve services that directly affect young people
- Cultivate future leaders

A step-by-step guide for establishing a youth council can be found at www.civics.org/resources/docs/Creating_a_Youth_Council_Final.pdf.

> ## Engaging Youth—It Works
>
> Youth who have had a government official in their classroom
> - Report higher levels of trust in local government
> - Are more likely to consider a job in government
>
> Youth who are involved in their communities
> - Have more positive views about government
> - Have a better understanding of how government works
>
> *Source*: North Carolina Civic Education Consortium, *Measures of Citizenship: The North Carolina Civic Index* (UNC School of Government, 2003)

> ## In Their Own Words: How to Engage Young People
>
> - Reach out to students who are not already engaged, not just the "usual suspects"
> - Offer students real world experiences
> - Be hands-on—learn about youth issues
> - Be visible
> - Make sure opportunities for youth are active
>
> *Source*: North Carolina Civic Education Consortium, *Measures of Citizenship: The North Carolina Civic Index* (UNC School of Government, 2003)

North Carolina Youth Councils: Two Examples

North Carolina boasts many successful youth councils. Some are city-wide, some are county-wide, and some are joint city/county endeavors. Some youth councils are housed in parks and recreation departments, some are overseen by a public information officer, and some operate jointly with cooperative extension. There is no one model for a successful youth council. Before a locality establishes a youth council, it is important to delineate desired outcomes for the council and create a structure that will support those outcomes. Two of North Carolina's many excellent youth councils are described below.

City of Sanford/Lee County Youth Council. The City of Sanford/Lee County Youth Council's mission is to represent the views and needs of Sanford and Lee County's young people to local decision makers. The youth council helps high school students gain an understanding of and appreciation for local government's impact on their everyday lives. The twelve council members are selected through a competitive application process. To be eligible, one must be enrolled in a high school in Lee County and have a minimum 2.3 grade point average (GPA).

The youth council meets once a month, and meetings are open to any young person who would like to observe and become involved. Some of the council's recent initiatives included hosting a youth summit, distributing and reading books to first graders in Lee County, organizing a downtown litter sweep, taking part in summer internships with local government, and volunteering with Kids Voting Lee County.

Hickory Youth Council. The Hickory Youth Council serves as the advisory council to the Hickory City Council, and members are charged with representing all youth residing within the City of Hickory. The council's twenty-five members are selected through a competitive application process. To be eligible, students must be high school–aged, must live in the City of Hickory or its extraterritorial jurisdiction, and must commit to maintaining and/or improving their GPAs while serving on the council.

The youth council meets on the second day of the month between September and May at various city facilities. The meetings are open to the public, and all are invited to attend. In addition to serving as an advisory council to the city council, members serve on other city boards and commissions, such as the community appearance commission and library advisory board; participate in community service projects; and hold events that build leadership skills for themselves and their peers.

If a locality is not ready to establish a youth council but seeks to reach out to young people, officials can encourage schools and community organizations to involve youth in simulations of city council and/or board of county commissioners meetings. When linked to school curriculum and broader learning objectives, these simulations provide youth with tangible examples of how local government affects their lives. Officials can become involved in these simulations by serving as resource people.

Older Residents

With the general aging of the U.S. population, there continue to be ever-increasing numbers of active senior citizens. Seniors often have deep roots in the community and can provide perspective on current issues. However, reaching older residents can be challenging.

The local Area Agency on Aging may be able to identify organizations that reach seniors in various ways. Some civic and social clubs and church groups can be good resources for reaching senior citizens. Also, older residents' growing use of e-mail and the Internet provides additional ways for contacting this segment of the community. These methods of outreach can be particularly useful given that issues affecting participation from this group can include lack of access to transportation and difficulty attending evening meetings.

A clearinghouse for how to reach older residents is available at www.dhhs.state.nc.us/aging/ aaa.htm.

People Who Are Often Away from Home

Some people refrain from participating in community affairs due to long commutes or time-consuming work obligations. Others may spend a large part of their time in another location, such as a vacation home or the home of a relative. Reaching these residents can be difficult.

Here are some ideas for reaching people who are on the move:

- Send periodic flyers or newsletters to their mailing addresses.
- Post information on a prominent billboard in your community, preferably near a main road used by commuters.
- Contact workplaces where travelling is central to many employees' work (for example, trucking companies, marketing and sales offices, consulting groups, and taxi companies).
- Use online social media, a listserv, or a voluntary e-mail notification system to reach people wherever they have Internet access.

Building Long-Term Capacity for Public Participation

A common complaint is that aside from voting in elections, the public only gets involved in short-term concerns and does not help elected officials address big-picture and long-term issues. This section examines the need to encourage public participation and provide specific steps to help citizens participate in government and become prospective leaders.

Building citizenship skills for people of all ages is important. Beyond voting and campaigning, what avenues are available for people to become involved in civic life? How well a plan for outreach and inclusion is developed and implemented will affect counties and cities in a variety of ways.

Public participation is greatly affected by the following factors:

- Involvement in voluntary civic affairs—church, scouting, nonprofit service groups, and so forth. People who are active in city or county issues often have volunteer experience in other groups.
- Involvement in local issues and how well (or poorly) those efforts are received by community leaders.

Three key parts of building capacity for public involvement are discussed below.

Providing Information

Getting information to the public is vital to increasing the level of public participation. State law mandates posting or mailing board meeting agendas and minutes to residents and media representatives. With fewer people reading newspapers, reaching residents is becoming more challenging. Local officials need to consider how to effectively provide information to residents. Table 3 sets forth the pros and cons of different methods of distributing information.

Table 3. Pros and Cons of Publicity Methods

Publicity Method	Pros	Cons
Newspaper announcements	Familiar Required for legal notices Reaches involved/educated residents	Declining readership in many places Hard for people to find; easy to skip over
County/city website	Easy Relatively inexpensive Full control of information	Limited readership People not aware when new material is posted Not everyone has Internet access
Community groups	Can target communication geographically or based on the issue Can reach members by phone, e-mail, etc.	May not be publicized to all interested people Lack of control—information may be edited or interpreted before it reaches members
Radio or TV public service announcements	Easy to write the announcement and contact station Radio and TV have public service obligations	Effectiveness depends how often and when announcement airs
Utility bill inserts	Full control of information Certain distribution Reaches many parts of the community	Can be overlooked or seen as junk May not reach residents of nursing homes or apartment complexes where utilities are paid by landlord
Postcard or newsletter produced by the government	Can target entire community or specific areas Full control of information	Expensive Timeliness may be an issue Bulk mail requires preparation to reduce costs Can be overlooked or seen as junk
E-mail (including listservs)	Easy Fast Familiar communication form for many residents	Requires people to provide their e-mail addresses Concerns about privacy or overuse Not everyone has Internet access
Social media such as Facebook, Myspace, Twitter	Easy Inexpensive Easy to cross-post from city/county official website	Depends on people signing up or becoming fans Not everyone has Internet access

Presenting Opportunities and Incentives

What opportunities exist for participation? And how will people be rewarded for participating?

Some possible incentives/rewards are

- Certificates
- Invitations to board meetings for special recognition
- Thank-you meals with one or more elected board members
- Photos displayed on the government website, in the newspaper, or in other locations
- Thank-you notes from the mayor or board
- Most importantly, clear evidence of the ways in which participants' work was used or their ideas implemented by the local government

Citizenship Skills

In the past, civics teaching often involved student councils and committees learning how to conduct meetings, debate resolutions, and hold elections. Now, the focus is on three skills for building long-term capacity for public involvement. Each of these skills is discussed below.

Understanding Different Views

Keeping an open mind is an important skill for elected officials (and for involved citizens and community leaders). It is easy to say and hard to practice. Acceptance of and respect for different values, opinions, and proposals is essential in a democracy. Meaningful policy is based on consideration of many different points of view. Providing opportunities for constituents to describe differing views is a critical skill.

Listening

Understanding people and their perspectives depends on good listening skills. Showing interest, paying attention, summarizing a person's view, and reading the person's body language are important parts of good listening. Refraining from interrupting or showing displeasure with a person's view sounds simple but is often very hard to do.

Seeking Some Area of Agreement for Common Action

Being able to compromise is an important aspect of working on public issues. After listening and being sure they understand different viewpoints, leaders need to work on creating options for action that can satisfy many of the concerns people express.

Activities and Programs for Building Long-Term Capacity

Although many programs for learning about government are designed for young people, most adults can benefit from more information about their local governments as well. Several North Carolina communities have citizen academies, where people can learn about what local government does (see sidebar). These programs range from one to as many as ten sessions and can involve field trips as well as information sharing in a classroom setting.

Cultivating More Informed Citizens

Across North Carolina, cities and counties large and small are sponsoring citizens academies (sometimes called "neighborhood colleges" or "Carolinaville 101") to help interested citizens learn more about how local government works. These programs are viewed not only as a way to educate citizens but also as a way to build and nurture positive relationships between citizens and local government. They can also help prepare people to serve on advisory boards or other positions within local government.

A typical academy in North Carolina involves several two-hour sessions, with groups of ten to twenty-five residents, and covers the wide range of activities of the city or county. These education sessions often involve field trips to such places as a water plant or a fire station. Citizens get to see how their city or county is run and get to meet the people who run it. At the end of the program, the citizens are recognized for their participation. For more information on citizens academies, see www.sog.unc.edu/programs/citizensacademies.

PART 2
Making Public Participation Happen

Guidance and Tips for Common Forms of Public Participation

Part 1 examined several issues public leaders should consider in choosing among various participation methods. This section offers guidance on ways to encourage public participation.

The following methods are often mandated by law and are used frequently:

- Public comment periods at board meetings
- Public hearings
- Community meetings
- Standing citizen advisory committees

The following methods are also sometimes used:

- Short-term advisory committees or task forces to address specific topics
- Public opinion surveys
- Blogs and social media

Each method is discussed below.

Public Comment Periods at Board Meetings

For school boards, city councils, and county commissions, common practice and state law dictate that people attending regular meetings of the elected board must have a chance to address the board (see sidebar on page 36). The legal standard is to have a public comment period at one meeting per month. If a board has more than one meeting per month, it is not required to have a public comment period at each meeting.[3]

The strengths of this type of participation are that it is open to all and each speaker chooses the topic that he or she will address. This open forum provides maximum control by the speakers, while a time limit for each speaker can be set by the board in order to treat speakers equally and manage the meeting effectively. A three-minute time limit is common. The board can also set other standards, such as no personal attacks, no obscene or vulgar language, and so forth.

The board must make a decision about where to place the citizen comment period in its meeting. Here are four options:

- Allow comments at the start of the meeting. This allows the board to hear concerns prior to action on any topic. Speakers make their points and can then depart if they wish (this is considered courteous to the speakers). However, speakers may not have all the information that the board has on a topic for that meeting, and thus the comments may not be as useful. Speakers may be frustrated if their views are at odds with what the board decides later in the meeting.
- Allow comments at the end of the meeting. This allows speakers to witness the board's decisions and actions prior to addressing the board. However, if the meeting is lengthy, speakers may be tired or frustrated by having to wait until the end.
- Allow comments on nonagenda issues only. This gives staff and commissioners the opportunity to conduct research and respond to comments appropriately at a later meeting. It may also alert commissioners to topics that could become major issues.
- Allow comments on a particular agenda item. This option would be *in addition to* a general comment period at the beginning or end of the meeting.

Here are suggested formats for multiple comment periods:

- Announce that there will be more than one comment period.
- For an agenda item, limit comment to viewpoints and information relevant to that topic only. Other comments must be reserved for the general comment period.
- Have the chair or another board member offer a summary of all the comments from speakers.

Tips for Making Public Comment Periods Effective

- *Share important materials with people in the audience.* Be sure everyone has a copy of the agenda and, if possible, copies of other materials the board will have. If printed copies are not available, a projector can be used to display some of the materials. If people sign up in advance and provide the clerk with phone numbers or e-mail addresses, some items can be sent to speakers in advance of the meeting. Agendas and materials can also be placed on the city's or county's website in advance of meetings.

- *Set and adhere to reasonable rules.* Common and acceptable restrictions include time limits for each speaker, a requirement that the speaker address the full board rather than an individual member, and a ban on criticism of employees (although there must be a procedure for such grievances to be heard in some other way). It is also reasonable and important to require the use of appropriate and respectful language. Some people may come to the meeting as a group and wish to designate individuals' floor time to a group spokesperson in order to allow one speaker more time to address a matter. A decision on whether to allow this approach should be made in advance of the meeting.

- *Listen carefully.* When board members look away, shuffle through papers, or even speak quietly among themselves while a speaker has the floor, it is almost always seen as disrespectful to the speaker. Such behavior should be avoided.

- *Be sure to thank each speaker.* Speakers are showing interest and concern for the community and are exercising their responsibilities as community members. Regardless of the speaker's viewpoint, such involvement should be acknowledged and encouraged.

- *Consider briefly summarizing each speaker's concerns.* A summary is one way of being an active listener and showing respect for people, especially when they are critical of board members or the board as a whole. It is important for speakers to know that their views are understood, even if they are not shared by all board members.

- *If the public is divided on an issue, make sure each side has an equal opportunity to address the governing board.* Create sheets on which people can sign up to speak for or against an issue and alternate speakers so that the audience and board members hear opposing points of view. Residents who are neutral or undecided should also be given the opportunity to sign up and speak.

Public Hearings

State laws mandate public hearings on a number of topics. The most common ones are local government land use decisions (such as rezonings and adoption or revision of comprehensive plans)[4] and annual budget adoptions (which require at least one public hearing prior to the board's vote).[5] However, city and county governing boards may choose to hold public hearings on any topic.

The statutes do not provide much information about how to conduct public hearings, and public officials often worry about their unpredictable nature. What if too few people participate or a single interest group dominates the hearing? What if a large and emotional crowd shows up and becomes contentious? Many of these worries can be lessened or avoided by careful planning and organization.

Tips for Organizing a Public Hearing

- Provide an opportunity for initial statements from two or more people with different viewpoints, followed by a roundtable discussion by three to six participants with different views. Allow the board members to ask questions and offer thoughts during the discussion.
- Identify people who share the same viewpoint (you can ask for a show of hands and allow one or two spokespersons extra time if people who have the same view clearly indicate that preference).

- Before speakers start, display flip chart pages with particular topics or issues that the board or staff members have identified as important in reaching a decision. As speakers make their points, have someone summarize each proposal or criticism under the appropriate topic.
- Hold a community workshop immediately before the public hearing. Provide information sheets and displays to allow people to take their time and look, read, and consider. Have staff experts present to listen and respond to people's concerns. Board members may also observe or participate as much as they desire, since the activity it is not part of the formal hearing. This period of informal give-and-take can help everyone understand the information and the different points of view, and board members can refer to what they learned at the workshop at the beginning of the formal hearing.

Community Meetings

In addition to formal public hearings that are set and guided by government officials, many elected officials participate in other group meetings or discussions. A city or county can sponsor its own community meeting with more informal or flexible arrangements.

Whereas a traditional public hearing only presents information, a community meeting allows for a more consultative approach. In such a setting, participants can share information and viewpoints, and questions can be asked and answered. The focus can be more on dialogue, rather than on specific proposals or demands of stakeholders.

There are a variety of ways to set up a community meeting. The expected size of the audience is one important factor in determining how to organize the meeting. Community meetings can take the following forms:

- Small groups, very informal, seated around tables for an open discussion
- Formal presentations followed by an opportunity for the public to question local government officials and board members
- Debates between representatives of opposing viewpoints, to which the board members are expected to listen and respond
- Gatherings to advocate singular viewpoints (for example, the need for better law enforcement in a specific neighborhood), where the group wants specific action by a board member or the whole board

Table 4. Community Meetings—Pros and Cons

Pros	Cons
Demonstrate responsiveness and willingness to meet people at a time/location convenient for them	Audience usually focused on a single neighborhood or composed of people sharing a similar characteristic or viewpoint
Informality allows for more interaction	Can be hard to control or could be inconclusive because there are no clear expectations or rules
Not government controlled	May not be publicized to all interested people
Flexibility allows individual board members to attend	Board members who are absent miss out on information and viewpoints Audience may expect action when only the full board can implement a policy shift or commit resources
Civic or social groups make the arrangements	Local groups have different skill levels in organizing meetings
Focus is on issues important to the community or local government	Some groups of attendees may wish to discuss other issues and highjack the conversation

Potential sponsors or organizers of community meetings include

- Social and civic clubs
- Churches and other religious organizations
- Formal or informal neighborhood groups or networks
- Business and professional organizations

Holding meetings in the community where people live and work can be helpful, but it can also pose challenges. Table 4 presents some of the pros and cons of community meetings.

Standing Citizen Advisory Committees

The majority of cities and counties in North Carolina use citizen advisory committees (CACs) to involve residents in local government. For counties, some committees—such as boards for health, social services, and mental health—are mandated by state statute and have significant powers. As cities adopt certain rules or begin providing certain services, they are required to create advisory boards for planning, alcoholic beverage control, and other purposes. However, most local government citizen advisory committees are optional and are created to advise city and county leaders on a variety of issues, such as environmental protection, economic development, transportation, and parks and recreation.

Whether or not to establish a CAC depends upon a local government's need for citizen involvement. Typically, CACs are more appropriate for complex, long-term issues affecting multiple interest groups, while straightforward issues affecting fewer people can be handled through targeted surveys or focus groups.

Standing CACs have a wide range of possible benefits and costs, and it is important for local governments to understand the reasons for creating advisory committees and the best ways to go about doing so. For more information—including a model policy for establishing CACs—see the separate *Board Builders* publication, *Creating and Maintaining Effective Local Government Citizen Advisory Committees*, by Vaughn Mamlin Upshaw.

Short-Term Committees or Task Forces to Address Specific Topics or Issues

Having a group take time to consider an important topic or issue is one way of adding depth to public participation. Participants are encouraged to engage and collaborate with each other and with local officials. Such groups are also a good way to involve residents with different interests, backgrounds, and skills, as well as those residents who are unable to commit to serving on long-term standing committees. It should be noted, however, that groups may require significant staff time and effort (see sidebar on page 40).

Tips for Establishing Short-Term Committees or Task Forces

- *Provide a clear, limited focus for the group's work and desired outcome.* For example, instead of asking the group to recommend what adult and youth recreation programs should look like in five years, ask the group to address specific questions, such as "Can we meet the demand for adult and youth recreation with current ball fields and playing space, or do we need expanded facilities?" and "If expansion is needed, what are the options and costs?"

- *Set a deadline for the group's recommendation or report to the board.* A two-to four-month time frame is optimal. Also keep in mind that participation often drops off during the winter holidays and in the summer.

- *Consider the balance of the group in terms of viewpoint, age, gender, length of residence in the community, and other factors.* It is easy to enlist highly motivated people to volunteer and advocate for their ideas. Consider setting a ground rule that all participants must approach the topic with an open mind. If possible, recruit

> ## Ad Hoc Citizen Groups and Staffing
>
> **Groups will require more time** for staff to work between meetings and provide guidance so that meetings are productive when they involve
>
> 1. Many members (eight or more)
> 2. Strong advocates (will require staff time to gather unbiased information and help people discuss their viewpoints rationally)
> 3. Evening or weekend meetings
> 4. Complicated topics
> 5. New topics or issues on which people are still making up their minds
> 6. Areas in which staff members do not have expertise
> 7. Chairs who are not strong leaders or do not have much time to help with research and communicating with members between meetings
>
> **Groups will require less staff time** when they involve
>
> 1. Few members (eight or fewer)
> 2. Open-minded members who do not hold strong, opposing viewpoints
> 3. Daytime meetings
> 4. Clear, limited topics
> 5. Familiar situations or topics, so that members have a good starting point
> 6. Areas in which staff have expertise (however, members may want external information or opinions as well)
> 7. Chairs who are strong leaders and can devote time to helping with research and communicating with members between meetings

residents who are thoughtful and concerned about the overall welfare of the town, county, or community but do not have a specific solution in mind.

- *Allocate resources for staffing and information needs.* Members of an ad hoc group need good information to be effective. This will often come from existing documents held by the county or city, but it may also require research by employees or external consultants.

- *Appoint a liaison between the group and the board.* It is often good to have a board member either participate in the temporary group or serve as the liaison between the group and the board. This person should be able to offer timely feedback without controlling the group. Sometimes a staff member can serve in this role, but it is usually best for an elected official to address questions about the political feasibility of options the group considers. The person in this role should be able to confirm the scope and goals of the short-term group and help the group prepare and evaluate a list of alternatives for dealing with the issue at hand.

- *Show appreciation to the people who contributed their time and talent.* The board can thank the group directly at a public meeting, or it may choose to send each group member a note or a small gift as appropriate.

Public Opinion Surveys

Several organizations conduct general surveys of opinion on statewide issues. Surveys are often related to campaigns and elections or to national or state policy matters. Surveys can also provide useful information to local governments.

A few North Carolina communities conduct general surveys to elicit the public's views about government services and to learn about current concerns. These surveys usually use sampling techniques to assure that a representative group is contacted. Creating a representative sample involves a significant investment of time and money. Most cities and counties are reluctant to incur that expense.

Examples of surveys used by North Carolina local governments are available at www.sog.unc.edu/programs/citizensurveys.

To avoid the high cost of random sample surveys, some communities conduct surveys via inserts in utility bills, through purchased ads in newspapers, or by asking residents to respond to questions on the Internet. These methods are cheaper and easier and can provide some useful information, but they run the risk of yielding results that do not reflect the opinions of the general community.

Either method of polling can address three important issues for local government boards: planning, budgeting, and evaluation. Planning surveys ask what people want in the way of physical improvements, public facilities, and services. Budgeting surveys explore respondents' priorities in terms of taxes and services. Evaluation questions seek feedback on the quality of the services the local government provides.

Surveys benefit local governments by

- Allowing the local government to obtain information on the views of many people rather than just hearing from small groups of residents with strong opinions on an issue
- Addressing more than one topic at a time (or two to three "hot" topics)
- Demonstrating local government's interest in the general public's opinion on issues
- Providing an easy way to compare information gathered at different times

Tips for Designing Local Government Surveys

- Carefully select questions that can be easily understood by a wide range of citizens
- Have a clear method for assuring a representative sample (see the sidebar on page 41 for a link to surveys used by North Carolina municipalities and the Appendix for resources on conducting surveys)
- Ensure that results can and will be communicated to participants and the wider community
- Be prepared for results that may not match board members' and officials' views on what is best for the community
- Expect that some people who take the survey will not understand the questions or may have opinions that are based on incomplete or misleading information

Blogs and Social Media

Blog is short for "web log"—a webpage where people share their opinions and personal news. Blogs and other Internet sites that allow people to share personal information, photographs, videos, and so forth are collectively termed "social media." Myspace, Facebook, Twitter, and YouTube are examples of social media.

Some North Carolina local governments are using social media to share information and respond to residents' concerns. This rapidly growing form of communication is also rapidly changing.

Social Media for Citizen Participation: North Carolina Examples and General Best Practices *is available at www.sog.unc.edu/wresources/socialmedia-citpartic/index.php.*

An elected official has several options for the use of social media (see sidebar, above). He or she can do any of the following:

- Refrain from blogging or posting views on other blogs or social media. Anything posted is considered public, and there are other, better ways to share views and interact with constituents.
- Participate in other people's blogs by posting comments there, without being responsible for maintaining the blog and creating new material. As long as it is a nongovernmental blog, there are no public records issues. The official can choose how and when to comment, and posting comments may elicit requests from the blog's readers for further responses.

- Have his or her own blog (see tips below). However, if part of the purpose of the blog is to conduct public business (and especially if government-owned equipment or software is used), the blog is likely to be a public record under the law.
- Monitor the jurisdiction's blogs or other social media in order to access information and public comment. These blogs fall under the public records law and may create a limited forum for public comment.

Tips for Blogging

Blogs are designed for people to post viewpoints. Posts vary in depth, civility, and type of topic addressed.

If you wish to blog, consider taking the following steps:

1. Find out who is blogging about your county or city government or community issues.

2. Use Google Alerts [www.google.com/alerts?hl=en] and enter the name of the jurisdiction and/or the elected official(s) name(s). Google Alerts will provide a summary of all web postings about a given topic or person each day via e-mail. Also, HootSuite [http://hootsuite.com] and TweetDeck [www.tweetdeck.com] can be used to monitor "mentions" on various forms of social media. Many local governments use these resources to manage their social media presence as well as to monitor information being shared about them.

3. Comment on someone else's blog. You are free to state your views in response to the opinions of people in the community.

4. Create your own blog.

   A. Decide whether it will be a personal blog focused on your political concerns or a government blog representing the city or county elected board.
   - If you establish a personal blog, your views are more likely to be seen as political. Government blogs are viewed as more nonpartisan. First Amendment and public records issues are more likely to arise in connection with a government-operated blog.
   - Be aware, however, that some content on a personal blog may be considered a public record.

   B. Be clear and authentic. If someone writes a blog post under your name, be clear about who has done it or who is assisting you. Blog etiquette places a high value on transparency and honesty.

   C. Plan on a regular commitment of time and attention. You should post a comment at least once or twice a week to keep people interested in your blog

D. Set standards about replies to your posts. One option is to set the software not to allow comments by others. If you wish to allow comments, you should take the following steps:

- Establish a standard for ensuring that people from your community are commenting, such as requiring entry of a zip code.
- State your expectations for participation in your blog, such as a focus on official actions, no obscenity, no personal attacks, and so forth.
- Refuse to allow anonymous postings.

Conclusion

This guide offers practical tips for public participation in city and county government. Engaging the public goes beyond tips and tools, however. As the discussion of the whys and whens of public participation demonstrated, the vast majority of public participation in local government is at the discretion of public officials. The extent to which officials engage the public and the forms that engagement takes are based upon the culture of the community, the tradition and capacity of the local government, and the values and priorities of the governing board. Regardless of the approach the board takes, its direction should be purposeful, and decisions on when, how, and why to invite public participation should be based on informed discussion that considers the issues addressed here.

Appendix: Resources

UNC School of Government (SOG)

General Public Participation Resources: www.sog.unc.edu/programs/participation/index.html

N.C. Civic Education Consortium, *Guide for Creating a Local Government Youth Council*: www.sog.unc.edu/programs/civiced/resources/docs/Creating_a_Youth_Council_Final.pdf

Citizen Participation and Social Media—General Resources:

Tufts, Shannon, and John Stephens. *Social Media for Citizen Participation* (June 2010): www.sog.unc.edu/wresources/socialmedia-citpartic/

Legal Dimensions of Using Social Media in Government:

Bluestein, Frayda. "Citizen Participation Information as Public Record." In *Coates' Canons*, April 14, 2010: http://sogweb.sog.unc.edu/blogs/localgovt/

Bluestein, Frayda. "Free Speech Rights in Government Social Media Sites." In *Coates' Canons*, March 3, 2010: http://sogweb.sog.unc.edu/blogs/localgovt/

School of Government Resource Page on Citizens Academies (including information on North Carolina communities conducting citizens academies): www.sog.unc.edu/programs/citizensacademies

Selected SOG Publications
For details, see www.sog.unc.edu, "Publications."

Citizens' Involvement:

Berner, Maureen, and John Stephens. "Article 9: Citizens' Involvement." In *County and Municipal Government in North Carolina*, Chapel Hill, NC: UNC School of Government, 2007.

Public Opinion Surveys:

Berner, Maureen, Ashley Bowers, and Laura Heyman. "So you want to do a survey . . ." *Popular Government* 67, no. 4 (2002): 23–32.

Public Comment at Elected Board Meetings:

Stephens, John, and A. Fleming Bell, II. "Public Comment at Business Meetings of Local Government Boards, Part One: Guidelines for Good Practices." *Popular Government* 62, no. 4 (1997).

Bell, A. Fleming, II, John Stephens, and Christopher Bass. "Public Comment at Business Meetings of Local Government Boards, Part Two: Common Practices and Legal Standards." *Popular Government* 63, no. 1 (1997).

Other Resources

International Association for Public Participation, *IAP2's Public Participation Toolbox*: http://iap2.affiniscape.com/associations/4748/files/06Dec_Toolbox.pdf

National League of Cities, *Programs and Services: Democratic Governance*: www.nlc.org/resources_for_cities/programs___services/697.aspx

Institute for Local Government, *Public Engagement and Collaborative Governance*: www.ca-ilg.org/engagement. Includes links to the following articles:

"A Local Official's Guide to Public Engagement in Budgeting"
"Planning Public Forums: Questions to Guide Local Officials"
"Getting the Most Out of Public Hearings: A Guide to Improve Public Involvement"

Public Opinion Surveys: A free, online booklet explaining mail and telephone surveys and focus groups is available from the American Statistical Association: www.amstat.org/sections/srms/pamphlet.pdf

Study Circles: More information is available from Everyday Democracy: www.everyday-democracy.org

Notes

1. Pew Research Center for the People & the Press, *Public Trust in Government: 1958–2010, available at* http://people-press.org/trust/.
2. See Vaughn Mamlin Upshaw, *Creating and Maintaining Effective Local Government Citizen Advisory Committees* (UNC School of Government, 2010).
3. Sections 153A-52.1 (counties) and 160A-81.1 (cities) of the North Carolina General Statutes (hereinafter G.S.).
4. G.S. 153A-323 (counties); G.S. 160A-364 (cities).
5. G.S. 159-12.